Summary

This report provides an overview of U.S. foreign assistance to Israel. It includes a review of past aid programs, data on annual assistance, and an analysis of current issues. For general information on Israel, see CRS Report RL33476, *Israel: Background and Relations with the United States*, by Carol Migdalovitz. For information on overall U.S. assistance to the Middle East, see CRS Report RL32260, *U.S. Foreign Assistance to the Middle East: Historical Background, Recent Trends, and the FY2011 Request*, by Jeremy M. Sharp.

Israel is the largest cumulative recipient of U.S. foreign assistance since World War II. From 1976-2004, Israel was the largest annual recipient of U.S. foreign assistance, having since been supplanted by Iraq. Since 1985, the United States has provided nearly $3 billion in grants annually to Israel.

Almost all U.S. bilateral aid to Israel is in the form of military assistance. In the past, Israel also had received significant economic assistance. Strong congressional support for Israel has resulted in Israel's receiving benefits not available to other countries. For example, Israel can use some U.S. military assistance both for research and development in the United States and for military purchases from Israeli manufacturers. In addition, all U.S. foreign assistance earmarked for Israel is delivered in the first 30 days of the fiscal year. Most other recipients normally receive aid in installments. Congress also appropriates funds for joint U.S.-Israeli missile defense programs.

In August 2007, the Bush Administration announced that it would increase U.S. military assistance to Israel by $6 billion over the next decade. The agreement calls for incremental annual increases in Foreign Military Financing (FMF) to Israel, reaching $3 billion a year by FY2011.

For FY2011, the Obama Administration requested $3 billion in FMF to Israel. According to the State Department's FY2011 budget justification for Foreign Operations, "U.S. assistance will help ensure that Israel maintains its qualitative military edge over potential threats, and prevent a shift in the security balance of the region. U.S. assistance is also aimed at ensuring for Israel the security it requires to make concessions necessary for comprehensive regional peace."

After years of negotiation, the United States and Israel announced in August 2010 that Israel will purchase 20 F-35s at a cost of $2.75 billion, which will be paid for entirely with FMF grants. The first planes are scheduled to be delivered in 2015, though the deal is still pending final approval by the Israeli cabinet.

Contents

Tables

Appendixes

Contacts

Developments in 2010

Loan Guarantees

In a January 2010 PBS interview, Charlie Rose asked President Obama's Special Envoy for Middle East Peace, former Senator George Mitchell, to comment on the possible use of U.S. punitive measures against Israel should the Administration not receive Israeli cooperation on peacemaking/halting settlement construction. Mitchell responded by stating:

> Under American law, the United States can withhold support on loan guarantees to Israel. President George W. Bush did so.... That's one mechanism that's been publicly discussed. There are others, and you have to keep open whatever options. But our view is that we think the way to approach this is to try to persuade the parties what is in their self-interest. And we think that we are making some progress in that regard and we're going to continue in that effort, and we think the way to do it is to get them into negotiations.

In response, Israeli Finance Minister Yuval Steinitz remarked that "We don't have to use those guarantees. We are doing very well without them."[1] Senator Joseph Lieberman added that "Any attempt to pressure Israel, to force Israel to the negotiating table by denying Israel support, will not pass in Congress.... Congress will act against any attempt to do that. I don't think it will come to this point."

Iron Dome

In March 2010, the Obama Administration announced that it would support $205 million in defense assistance to Israel for the purchase of up to ten Iron Dome batteries.[2] If passed, H.R. 5136, the National Defense Authorization bill for Fiscal Year 2011, would authorize the full $205 million for Israel's procurement of Iron Dome. The Senate's companion bill, S. 3454, also would authorize the full amount. In May 2010, the House passed H.R. 5327, United States-Israel Rocket and Missile Defense Cooperation and Support Act, which authorized the Administration "to provide assistance to the Government of Israel for the procurement, maintenance, and sustainment of the Iron Dome Short Range Artillery Rocket Defense System for purposes of intercepting short-range rockets, missiles, and mortars launched against Israel." A Senate version of this bill, S. 3451, awaits floor action.

F-35 Aircraft

After years of negotiation, the United States and Israel announced in August 2010 that Israel will purchase 20 F-35s at a cost of $2.75 billion, which will be paid for entirely using FMF grants. The first planes are scheduled to be delivered in 2015, though the deal is still pending final

---

[1] Israel's economy has been steadily growing in recent years. Israel has not drawn on the loan guarantees since FY2004.

[2] Iron Dome is a short-range missile defense system designed to destroy crude Palestinian and Iranian-made mortars and rockets fired by militants from the Gaza Strip and southern Lebanon. For more information see, "Defense Budget Appropriations for U.S.-Israeli Missile Defense Programs."

approval by the Israeli cabinet. Prior to the agreement, both sides had negotiated over the level of Israeli customization of the F-35.

U.S.-Israeli Relations and the Role of Foreign Aid

For decades, the United States and Israel have maintained strong bilateral relations based on a number of factors, including strong domestic U.S. support for Israel; shared strategic goals in the Middle East (concern over Iran, Syria, Islamic extremism); shared democratic values; and historic ties dating from U.S. support for the creation of Israel in 1948. U.S. foreign aid has been a major component in cementing and reinforcing these ties. Although there have been occasional differences over Israel's settlements in the West Bank and Gaza Strip (prior to the 2005 disengagement) and Israeli arms sales to China, successive Administrations and many lawmakers have long considered Israel to be a reliable partner in the region, and U.S. aid packages for Israel have reflected this sentiment.

U.S. military aid has helped transform Israel's armed forces into one of the most technologically sophisticated militaries in the world. U.S. military aid for Israel has been designed to maintain Israel's "qualitative military edge" (QME) over neighboring militaries, since Israel must rely on better equipment and training to compensate for a manpower deficit in any potential regional conflict. U.S. military aid, a portion of which may be spent on procurement from Israeli defense companies, also has helped Israel build a domestic defense industry, which ranks as one of the top 10 suppliers of arms worldwide.

For many years, U.S. economic aid helped subsidize a lackluster Israeli economy, though since the rapid expansion of Israel's hi-tech sector in the 1990s (sparked partially by U.S.-Israeli scientific cooperation), Israel is now considered a fully industrialized nation with an economy on par with some Western European countries. Consequently, Israel and the United States agreed to gradually phase out economic grant aid to Israel. In FY2008, Israel stopped receiving bilateral Economic Support Fund (ESF) grants. It had been a large-scale recipient of grant ESF assistance since 1971.

The use of foreign aid to help accelerate the Middle East peace process has had mixed results. The promise of U.S. assistance to Israel and Egypt during peace negotiations in the late 1970s enabled both countries to take the risks needed for peace, and may have helped convince them that the United States was committed to supporting their peace efforts. Promoting Israeli-Palestinian peace has proven to be a far greater challenge for U.S. policy makers, as most analysts consider foreign aid to be tangential to solving complex territorial issues and overcoming deeply rooted mistrust sown over decades.

Critics of U.S. aid policy, particularly some in the Middle East, argue that U.S. foreign aid exacerbates tensions in the region. Many Arab commentators insist that U.S. assistance to Israel indirectly causes suffering to Palestinians by supporting Israeli arms purchases. In the past, the United States reduced loan guarantees to Israel in opposition to continued settlement building, but it has not acted unilaterally to cut Israel's military or economic grant aid and has not made deductions to loan guarantees in some years.

Qualitative Military Edge (QME)

Congress has taken measures to strengthen Israel's security and maintain its "qualitative military edge" over neighboring militaries, and successive administrations have routinely affirmed the U.S. commitment to strengthening Israel's QME. For years, no official or public U.S. definition of QME existed.[3] In 2008, Congress passed legislation (P.L. 110-429, the Naval Vessel Transfer Act of 2008) that defines QME as:

> the ability to counter and defeat any credible conventional military threat from any individual state or possible coalition of states or from non-state actors, while sustaining minimal damage and casualties, through the use of superior military means, possessed in sufficient quantity, including weapons, command, control, communication, intelligence, surveillance, and reconnaissance capabilities that in their technical characteristics are superior in capability to those of such other individual or possible coalition of states or non-state actors.

Furthermore, Section 201 of the act requires the President to carry out an "empirical and qualitative assessment on an ongoing basis of the extent to which Israel possesses a qualitative military edge over military threats to Israel." It also further amends Section 36 of the Arms Export Control Act to require certifications for proposed arms sales "to any country in the Middle East other than Israel" to include "a determination that the sale or export of the defense articles or defense services will not adversely affect Israel's qualitative military edge over military threats to Israel."

Over the years, Israeli officials have expressed concern over U.S. sales of sophisticated weaponry, particularly aircraft, airborne radar systems, and precision-guided munitions, to Arab Gulf countries, notably Saudi Arabia. Arab critics of U.S. military aid to Israel routinely charge that Israeli officials exaggerate the threat posed by Israel's neighbors in order to justify calls for increased U.S. support. As the United States is one of the principal suppliers of defense equipment and training to both Israel and Saudi Arabia, U.S. policymakers and defense officials must carefully navigate commitments to both countries, including upholding the U.S. commitment to maintaining Israel's QME. The threat of a nuclear-armed Iran, though it has partially aligned Israeli and Sunni Arab interests in deterring a shared rival, also may be exacerbating Israeli fears of a deteriorated QME, as Saudi Arabia and other Gulf states dramatically increase defense procurements from U.S. and other foreign suppliers.

In the summer and fall of 2010, media reports indicated that the United States was on the verge of selling Saudi Arabia as many as 84 Boeing F-15 fighters (and upgrading the kingdom's existing fleet of 150 F-15s), helicopters, and upgrades to its naval forces in a deal valued as much as $60 billion. In order to assuage Israeli QME concerns, the fighters will reportedly lack "standoff systems," which are long-range weapons that can be used in offensive operations against land- and sea-based targets.[4] According to Pentagon Press Secretary Geoff Morrell, "We have been working very closely with the Israeli government at the highest levels to address their concerns on this and other issues…. Israel is not the only one with security concerns in the region and we have responsibilities to other allies as well." Unlike in years past, there is no indication of any major Israeli opposition to the proposed sale. Some analysts have suggested that the proposed F-15 configuration for Saudi Arabia, when combined with a possible Israeli purchase of the F-35 -

---

[3] William Wunderle and Andre Briere, *U.S. Foreign Policy and Israel's Qualitative Military Edge: The Need for a Common Vision*, Washington Institute for Near East Policy, Policy Focus #80, January 2008.

[4] "U.S. to Sell Fighter Jets to Saudis," *Wall Street Journal*, August 8, 2010.

the most advanced fighter in the world, should be sufficient enough to satisfy Israeli QME airpower concerns. Israeli Ambassador to the United States Michael Oren commented on the planned sale, saying "We appreciate the Administration's efforts to maintain Israel's qualitative military edge, and we expect to continue to discuss our concerns with the Administration about the issues."[5]

In July 2010, Assistant Secretary of State for Political-Military Affairs Andrew J. Shapiro publicly reaffirmed the Obama Administration's commitment to preserving Israel's QME. In his remarks, he stated that

> Each and every security assistance request from the Israeli Government is evaluated in light of our policy to uphold Israel's Qualitative Military Edge. At the same time, QME considerations extend to our decisions on defense cooperation with all other governments in the region. This means that as a matter of policy, we will not proceed with any release of military equipment or services that may pose a risk to allies or contribute to regional insecurity in the Middle East.... U.S. support for Israel's security is much more than a simple act of friendship. We are fully committed to Israel's security because it enhances our own national security and because it helps Israel to take the steps necessary for peace.[6]

U.S. Bilateral Military Aid to Israel

A 10-Year Military Aid Agreement

In August 2007, the Bush Administration announced that it would increase U.S. military assistance to Israel by $6 billion over the next decade. The agreement calls for incremental $150 million annual increases in FMF to Israel, starting at $2.55 billion in FY2009 and reaching $3 billion by 2011.[7] Under the terms of the agreement, Israel will still be able to spend 26% of U.S. assistance on Israeli-manufactured equipment. According to former Under Secretary of State for Political Affairs Nicholas Burns, who signed the Memorandum of Understanding on U.S. Military Assistance:

The Second 10-Year Plan: Proposed U.S. Military Aid to Israel FY2009-FY2018	
FY2009	$2.55 billion
FY2010	$2.77 billion
FY2011	$3.00 billion
FY2012-2018	$3.09 billion a year
Source: U.S. State Department	

> We consider this 30 billion dollars in assistance to Israel to be an investment in peace - in long-term peace. Peace will not be made without strength. Peace will not be made without Israel being strong in the future. Of course, our objective as a country and our specific objective as a government is to contribute to that peace, a peace between Israel and the Palestinian people, the creation of an independent Palestinian state willing to live side by

---

[5] "Saudi Arms Deal Advances ," *Wall Street Journal*, September 12, 2010.

[6] *The Obama Administration's Approach to U.S.-Israel Security Cooperation: Preserving Israel's Qualitative Military Edge*, U.S. State Department, Remarks at the Brookings Saban Center for Middle East Policy, July 16, 2010.

[7] During negotiations for the new aid agreement, Israel reportedly had wanted a larger portion of FMF up front. The Bush Administration insisted, however, that because there was limited additional funding in the foreign aid budget for large increases in military assistance, the United States lacked the fiscal flexibility to dramatically increase Israel's aid all at once. Ultimately, the Bush Administration's incremental approach won out.

side in peace with Israel, and a general peace in the region that has eluded the Israeli people for 59 years but which is, we hope, the destiny of the Israeli people as well as the Arab peoples of the region. Our policy in this entire region is dedicated to that final objective.[8]

Foreign Military Financing (FMF)

Early Transfer

Congress has mandated that Israel receive its FMF aid in a lump sum during the first month of the fiscal year. Once disbursed, Israel's military aid is transferred to an interest bearing account with the Federal Reserve Bank. Israel has used interest collected on its military aid to pay down its debt (non-guaranteed) to the United States, which, according to the U.S. Treasury Department, stood at $625 million as of August 2010.[9] Israel cannot use accrued interest for defense procurement inside Israel.

FMF for in-Country Purchase

Most analysts consider Israel's ability to use a significant portion of its annual military aid for procurement in Israel to be a valuable aspect of its assistance package; no other recipient of U.S. military assistance has been granted this benefit.[10] The proceeds to Israeli defense firms from purchases with U.S. funds have allowed the Israeli defense industry to achieve necessary economies of scale and produce highly sophisticated equipment for niche markets. Defense experts note that high annual amounts of U.S. military assistance force private and semi-private Israeli defense companies to place a greater business emphasis on exports, since a large portion of Israeli government weapons procurement is spent on American equipment. According to Beth McCormick, former acting director of the U.S. Defense Technology Security Administration, Israeli manufacturers must sell as much as 75% of their output abroad to stay profitable, a far higher share than U.S. military contractors.[11] Successive Administrations and many lawmakers believe that a strong domestic Israeli defense industry is crucial to maintaining Israel's technological edge over its neighbors. Israel is among the world's leading arms exporters. Between 2001 and 2008, Israel was the seventh-largest arms exporter to the world with sales

---

[8] R. Nicholas Burns, Under Secretary of State for Political Affairs, "Remarks and Press Availability at Signing Ceremony for Memorandum of Understanding on U.S. Military Assistance," Released by the American Embassy Tel Aviv – Press Section, August 16, 2007.

[9] CRS correspondence with U.S. Treasury Department.

[10] Israel was first granted FMF for use in Israel in 1977, when it asked for and received permission to use $107 million in FY1977 FMF funds to develop the Merkava tank (prototype completed in 1975 and added to Israeli arsenal in 1979). Several years later, Israel asked for a similar waiver to develop the Lavi ground-attack aircraft, and Congress responded with legislation allowing Israel to spend $250 million of FMF in Israel to develop the Lavi. It was estimated that the United States provided between $1.3 and $1.8 billion in Lavi development costs before the United States and Israel agreed to terminate the project in 1988. In order to defray the cancellation costs of the Lavi program, the United States agreed to raise the FMF earmark for procurement in Israel to $400 million. For background on the cancellation of the Lavi fighter, see Dan Raviv and Yossi Melman, *Friends in Deed: Inside the U.S.-Israeli Alliance*, New York: Hyperion, 1994, pp. 263-268.

[11] "Pentagon says Israel Improves Arms-Export Controls," *Reuters*, September 5, 2007.

(value of agreements not deliveries) worth a total of $9.9 billion.[12] In total, annual FMF grants to Israel represent 18.2% of the overall Israeli defense budget.[13]

Since FY1988, the FMF procurement earmark for purchases within Israel has been incorporated into annual foreign assistance legislation. Currently, approximately one quarter of Israel's FMF funds may be used for domestic defense purchases ($670.65 million in FY2009). As U.S. military aid to Israel has increased, the amount set aside for defense purchases in Israel also has increased.

Recent Congressional Notifications of Possible U.S. Military Sales to Israel

Israel uses almost 75% of its FMF funds to purchase U.S. defense equipment. By law, Congress must be notified of most new purchase agreements. The Department of Defense's Defense Security Cooperation Agency (DSCA) is charged with managing U.S. arms sales to Israel. Recent notifications include the following:

- On August 5, 2010, DSCA notified Congress of a possible Foreign Military Sale to Israel of unleaded gasoline, JP-8 aviation fuel, and diesel fuel. The total value of this deal is estimated at $2 billion.

In April 1998, the United States designated Israel as a "major non-NATO ally," which qualifies Israel to receive Excess Defense Articles (EDA) under Section 516 of the Foreign Assistance Act and Section 23(a) of the Arms Export Control Act. DSCA manages the EDA program, which enables the U.S. to reduce its inventory of outdated equipment by providing friendly countries with necessary supplies at either reduced rates or at no charge.[14]

The Costs and Benefits of Israeli Dependence on U.S. Weaponry

Although Israel's ability to spend FMF grants for off-shore procurement has significantly boosted its own defense industry, Israel still greatly relies on advanced U.S. weaponry to maintain its conventional superiority. For the most part, Israeli dependence on American equipment has been beneficial, though at times, some Israeli observers (like many other foreign recipients of U.S. aid), have expressed concern that U.S. military aid comes with its own conditions. Israel's defense establishment desires not only the most technologically advanced U.S. systems, but the knowledge to co-develop and integrate U.S. weaponry into its own defense architecture. Some Israelis bemoan the lack of U.S. support for co-research and development projects. According to Isaac Ben Israel, a former Member of the Knesset and Chairman of the Israel Space Agency:

> In contrast to practices of the past, Israel has not received any technological know-how from the Americans in recent years. Certainly Israel has received weapon systems from the US: combat systems, aircraft, electronic warfare systems, and various first line equipment of the highest quality of US technological production. But in recent years these items have arrived in sealed boxes that may not be opened; Israeli specialists may not know what is inside them

---

[12] CRS Report R41403, *Conventional Arms Transfers to Developing Nations, 2002-2009*, by Richard F. Grimmett

[13] "Highlights: Israel Economy News 14-20 Jun 09 (Israel—OSC Summary in English)," *Open Source Center*, June 20, 2009, GMP20090620739005.

[14] To access DSCA's Excess Defense Articles database, see http://www.dsca.mil/programs/eda/search.asp.

and occasionally oversight groups arrive to preclude the possibility that anything was opened illegally.[15]

The United States also maintains veto power over certain sales by Israel to third parties of defense equipment that may contain U.S. technology (see "Aid Restrictions and Possible Violations"), though some Israelis assert that export business is occasionally lost due to competition from American defense manufacturers.

Although FMF grants facilitate increased U.S.-Israeli military cooperation and weapons sales, purchase negotiations over sophisticated and expensive U.S. equipment can in some cases take years or fail altogether. Although overall cooperation remains robust, U.S.-Israeli arms sales agreements occasionally stumble due to disagreements over knowledge/technology transfer issues and cost. In certain cases, Israel may request that it be allowed to customize U.S. equipment to operate more smoothly with its own weapons systems. Israel also may seek the ability to independently maintain U.S. systems in case of emergencies.

Occasionally, negotiations stall over cost concerns. In 2009, Israel declined to purchase the Littoral Combat Ship manufactured by General Dynamics Corp. and Lockheed Martin Corp. due to its high cost and instead launched negotiations with a German company to buy several Meko Corvette warships.[16]

F-35 Joint Strike Fighter

For several years, Israel has sought to purchase as many as 75 F-35 Lightning II Fighters, the fifth generation stealth aircraft produced by the United States with research and assistance from eight other nations, including the United Kingdom, Canada, Denmark, The Netherlands, Norway, Italy, Turkey, and Australia. Although Israel and Singapore are not members of the F-35 cooperative development partnership, they are considered by the Pentagon to be "security cooperation participants" and have contributed $50 million each to development costs.

After years of negotiation, the United States and Israel announced in August 2010 that Israel will purchase 20 F-35s at a cost of $2.75 billion, which will be paid for entirely using FMF grants. The first planes are scheduled to be delivered in 2015, though the deal is still pending final approval by the Israeli cabinet. Prior to the agreement, both sides had negotiated over the level of Israeli customization of the F-35. Reportedly, a June 2010 Letter of Acceptance indicated that Israel will be able to install its own radio and datalink systems, and discussions over the integration of electronic warfare capabilities will continue and may be approved should Israel purchase additional planes.[17] As part of the deal, the United States agreed to make reciprocal purchases of equipment from Israel's defense industries estimated at $4 billion.[18]

---

[15] Isaac Ben Israel, *Israeli Security Dependence on the US*, Institute for National Security Studies, The US and Israel under Changing Political Circumstances, Tel Aviv, Israel, November 2009, pp. 75-79.

[16] "Israel Seeks Discount on Two German Warships," *Reuters*, November 25, 2009.

[17] "Defense Minister Barak approves purchase of 20 F-35 fighters for around $2.75 billion," *Ha'aretz*, August 16, 2010.

[18] "Israel set to build wings for some 800 F-35s," *Reuters*, August 30, 2010.

Defense Budget Appropriations for U.S.-Israeli Missile Defense Programs

Congress and successive Administrations have shown strong support for joint U.S.-Israeli missile defense projects. U.S.-Israeli missile defense cooperation has perennially been authorized and appropriated in the defense authorization and appropriations bills. Missile defense cooperation is generally not considered a form of direct aid, but many U.S. and Israeli observers consider it a vital component of the Israel's strategic relationship with the United States. Israel and the United States each financially contribute to several projects and share technology from co-developed weapons systems. The U.S. and Israeli militaries also participate together in joint biannual anti-aircraft exercises (code named Juniper-Cobra). According to various reports, the October 2009 Juniper-Cobra exercise included U.S. naval ships and ground personnel operating the Aegis, THAAD and Patriot missile shields in coordination with Israel's Arrow II interceptor. More than 1,000 U.S. troops participated in what was the largest U.S.-Israeli military exercise in history.

Multi-Layered Missile Defense

Over the past several years, U.S.-Israeli missile defense cooperation has evolved to include the co-development of several systems designed to thwart a diverse range of threats, from short-range missiles and rockets[19] fired by non-state actors, such as Hamas and Hezbollah,[20] to mid- and long-range ballistic missiles in Syria's and Iran's arsenals.[21] Israel also possesses U.S.-supplied Hawk and Patriot missile batteries. In addition to joint programs, Israel has its own missile defense programs.

---

[19] The "Qassam rocket," named after the early 20th century militant leader Shaikh Izz al Din al Qassam, is a rudimentary projectile welded from pipes and crude metals in the homes and workshops of Gazan engineers. It has a range of approximately 3 to 6 miles and is inaccurate. According to one account, Qassam rockets can be made for as little as $300 apiece using common items, such as fertilizer, sugar, and small amounts of gunpowder.

[20] Beginning in 1996, the United States and Israel funded a short-range, anti-rocket program called the Tactical High Energy Laser (THEL). Technical difficulties and financial disagreements with the prime contractor, TRW, over cost overruns plagued the program. Ultimately, after the United States and Israel invested between $300 and $400 million in the program ($139 million in U.S. contributions), defense experts concluded that the THEL prototype, although effective against rockets and mortars, was too expensive and immobile a solution. According to one analyst, "shooting the laser just once would have cost roughly $3,000, and that protecting the whole border of Israel would have required a few dozen of these systems." The program was terminated in September 2005, but was then revived a year later by Northrop Grumman which created "Skyguard," a more powerful version of the THEL.

Nevertheless, Israel's Ministry of Defense believes that Skyguard does not function optimally in bad weather. See, "U.S. and Israel Shelved Laser As a Defense," *New York Times*, July 30, 2006.

[21] In the mid-1990s, the U.S. Air Force analyzed alternatives for a theater missile defense system that could intercept missiles shortly after launch, when they are the most vulnerable. In June 1997, the United States and Israel began a joint research program to develop a fleet of unmanned aerial vehicles (UAVs) that could deliver weapons to intercept ballistic missiles immediately after launch (boost phase). In late 1999, apparently because of the complexities of the technology involved and disagreements between the United States and Israel over the potential merits of the system, Israel decided not to move toward full demonstration of the Boost Phase Intercept system. Congress provided a total of $53 million for the Boost Phase Intercept program.

Iron Dome

Israel has developed a short-range system, dubbed "Iron Dome," to destroy crude Palestinian and Iranian-made mortars and rockets fired by militants from the Gaza Strip and southern Lebanon. At least two Iron Dome batteries are expected to be deployed in November 2010 in the southern Negev desert. Iron Dome is designed to intercept very short-range threats between 2.5 and 45 miles in all-weather situations.[22] It was developed by Rafael Advanced Defense Systems.

For several years, the Israeli government sought U.S. assistance in financing the Iron Dome system. According to one Israeli defense official, "We're not just looking for funding assistance, although that is extremely important for us. We've offered the Americans to join as full participants and to use the system to defend their troops and assets around the world.... We're hopeful that after careful examination of the data and the system's capabilities, that they'll decide to join the program."[23]

In March 2010, the Obama Administration announced that it would support $205 million in defense assistance to Israel for the purchase of up to ten Iron Dome batteries. If passed, H.R. 5136, the National Defense Authorization bill for Fiscal Year 2011, would authorize the full $205 million for Israel's procurement of Iron Dome. The Senate's companion bill, S. 3454, also would authorize the full amount. In May 2010, the House passed H.R. 5327, United States-Israel Rocket and Missile Defense Cooperation and Support Act, which authorized the Administration "to provide assistance to the Government of Israel for the procurement, maintenance, and sustainment of the Iron Dome Short Range Artillery Rocket Defense System for purposes of intercepting short-range rockets, missiles, and mortars launched against Israel." A Senate version of this bill, S. 3451, awaits floor action.

Despite this new U.S. commitment, there are some Israeli concerns that a full nation-wide deployment of the Iron Dome system is too costly and may be insufficient to protect large metropolitan areas. Reportedly, each battery costs approximately $21 million, and some Israeli analysts suggest that at least 20 or more systems are needed to protect the most vulnerable northern and southern cities from mortar and rocket attacks.[24] Furthermore, firing a single Iron Dome interceptor could cost as much as $100,000.[25] Israel may plan to export the system to customers in Asia (such as Singapore and India) in order to recoup Iron Dome's cost.

According to the Israeli military, the system passed key tests in January and July 2010, though critics assert the system has difficulty intercepting mortar shells and Qassam rockets with a range

---

[22] Within the Israeli defense establishment, there is debate over how effective the Iron Dome system will be in protecting Israeli cities and towns from Palestinian Qassam and Katyusha rocket attacks fired from the Gaza Strip. Some Israeli defense experts assert that Iron Dome kinetic interceptors will take too long to destroy crude rockets fired from close range at Israeli towns such as Sderot. Reuven Pedazur, an Israeli expert in ballistic missiles, claims that each Tamir missile fired from the Iron Dome system will cost $100,000, while a system based on laser beam interception, would cost between $1,000 and $3,000 per strike. Nevertheless, Israeli officials argue that solid laser technology needs more time to develop. See, "Rocket, Missile Shields in Works; Iron Dome, David's Sling eye attacks from Gaza, Lebanon, Iran," *Washington Times*, August 8, 2008. According to one source, "Neither the missile interceptors nor the lasers will provide 100-percent coverage, which is why they will have to both be in use." See, "Defense Officials View Laser as Future of Anti-Missile Technology, *Ha'aretz*, March 24, 2008.

[23] "U.S. Eyes Joint Anti-Rocket Effort With Israel; Mulls $200M Investment To Speed Iron Dome,"*Agence France Presse*, June 9, 2008.

[24] "Jane's Missiles & Rockets," *Iron Dome Passes Final Development Tests*, August 2, 2010.

[25] Some estimates suggest that an interceptor may cost $50,000 per launch.

---

of 2.5 miles or less,[26] charging that its reaction time is too slow to effectively shoot down a Qassam rocket fired by Hamas close to the Israeli border.[27]

David's Sling

David's Sling (aka Magic Wand) is a short/medium-range system designed to counter long-range rockets and slower-flying cruise missiles, such as those possessed by Hezbollah in Lebanon, fired at ranges from 40 km to 300 km. It is being jointly developed by Israel's Rafael Advanced Defense Systems and Raytheon. The system is expected to be operational by 2010. In August 2008, Israel and the United States officially signed a "project agreement" to co-develop the David's Sling system. According to Lt. Gen. Henry Obering, director of the U.S. Missile Defense Agency, "We wanted a truly co-managed program because the United States will be very interested in this for our own purposes.... The agreement we just signed allows us to work through specific cost-sharing arrangements and other program parameters."[28]

The Arrow and Arrow II

Since 1988, Israel and the United States have been developing the Arrow Anti-Missile System, a weapon with a theater ballistic missile defense capability. The United States has funded just under half of the annual costs of the development of the Arrow Weapon System, with Israel supplying the remainder of the costs. The Arrow became operational in 2000. The Arrow II program, a joint effort of Boeing and Israel Aerospace Industries (IAI), is designed to defeat longer-range conventional ballistic missiles.

High Altitude Missile Defense System (Arrow-III)

Fearing a potential nuclear threat from Iran, Israel has sought a missile interceptor that operates at a higher altitude and greater range than the Arrow. In October 2007, the United States and Israel agreed to establish a committee to evaluate Israel's proposed "Arrow III," a top-tier system designed to intercept advanced missiles with nuclear-tipped warheads. The Arrow III will be a more advanced version—in terms of speed, range and altitude—of the current Arrow II interceptor. In the spring and summer of 2008, Israel decided to begin production of the Arrow III and the United States agreed to co-fund its development despite a proposal by Lockheed Martin urging Israel to purchase the Terminal High-Altitude Area Defense (THAAD) missile defense system. In 2009, some Israelis feared that U.S.-Israeli co-funding for the Arrow III would be eliminated and replaced by Raytheon's SM-3 interceptor found on Aegis warships. The SM-3 costs considerably more per missile than the Arrow III ($10-$12 million versus $1.5-$2 million).[29] The Arrow III is made by Israel Aerospace Industries (IAI) and Boeing. It is expected

---

[26] "Iron Dome may not be as Effective as the IDF Thinks," *Ha'aretz*, July 22, 2010.

[27] In 2009, reports surfaced suggesting that Israel had expressed an interest in purchasing the U.S. Vulcan-Phalanx cannon and radar system to shoot down mortars and rockets with a range under three miles. Manufactured by Raytheon, the Vulcan-Phalanx is currently deployed in Iraq and Afghanistan, but there have been no recent reports of U.S. sales of the system to Israel. One Vulcan-Phalanx unit reportedly costs $15 million though each unit can only defend a small area.

[28] "U.S.-Israel To Develop David's Sling Missile Defense," *DefenseNews.com*, August 7, 2008.

[29] According to Arrow designer Uzi Rubin, "The question is what's easier: to take a foreign-designed missile across the barriers of sovereignty and proprietary rights and somehow integrate it into our system, or to do it in-house? To do it in-house is cheaper and faster." See, "In Restive Med, U.S. Ship Eyes Risk of Missile War," *Reuters*, September 17, (continued...)

---

to be tested in 2011 and possibly deployed by 2014. In July 2010, the United States and Israel signed a bilateral agreement to extend their cooperation in developing and producing the Arrow III.

X-Band Radar

One of the most significant gestures of U.S. support for Israel's missile defense architecture has been the deployment of the AN/TPY-2 X-Band radar system (built by Raytheon Co.) to Israel in late 2008. Not only is the X-Band system far more capable of detecting incoming missiles than Israel's existing radar,[30] but the United States also has linked the X-Band to its global network of satellites in the U.S. Defense Support Program (DSP). The DSP is the principal component of the U.S. Satellite Early Warning System to detect missile launches.[31] According to various media reports, the X-Band system is now operational. It will remain U.S.-owned and operated by, for the first time ever, a constant presence of U.S. troops and defense contractors on Israeli soil. Reportedly, the system has been deployed to a secret location in the southern Negev desert close to the Egyptian border.

P.L. 110-417, the Duncan Hunter National Defense Authorization Act for Fiscal Year 2009, authorized up to $89 million for the activation and deployment of the AN/TPY-2 forward-based X-band radar to a "classified location."[32] According to the Section 236 of the act, U.S. funding may not be appropriated until the Secretary of Defense submits to the Committees on Armed Services of the Senate and the House of Representatives a report on the deployment of the X-band radar describing, among other things: the location of deployment of the radar; the operational parameters of the deployment of the radar; and the cost-sharing arrangements between the United States and the country in which the radar will be deployed.

(...continued)

2009.

[30] The X-Band system can detect incoming missiles from 500-600 miles. Currently, Israel's early warning system is only able to detect missiles from 100 miles out.

[31] Israel was first given access to DSP in 2001 but only on a per-request, rather than constant, basis.

[32] In report language (H.Rept. 110-652) accompanying H.R. 5658, the House-passed FY2009 Defense Authorization bill, Members stated that "The State of Israel faces a real and growing threat from short- and medium-range ballistic missiles from states such as the Syrian Arab Republic and the Islamic Republic of Iran. The committee believes that the deployment of a U.S. Army-Navy/Transportable-2 (AN/TPY-2) missile defense discrimination radar to Israel would greatly increase the capabilities of both Israel and U.S. forces deployed in support of Israel to defend against ballistic missile threats. Therefore, the committee urges the Department of Defense to begin discussions with Israel about the possibility of deploying an AN/TPY-2 radar on its territory at the earliest feasible date." The Senate version, S. 3001, included an amendment making funds available for the deployment of the AN/TPY-2 forward-based X-band radar.

**Table 1. Defense Budget Appropriations for U.S.-Israeli Missile Defense:
FY2006-FY2011 Request**

($ in millions)

System Type	FY2006	FY2007	FY2008	FY2009	FY2010	FY2011 Request
Short-Range (David's Sling)	$10.0	$20.4	$37.0	$72.895	$80.092	$47.0
Arrow (Arrow-2)	$122.866	$117.494	$98.572	$74.342	$72.306	$24.0
High Altitude (Arrow-3)	—	—	$20.0	$30.0	$50.036	$51.0
Total	**$132.866**	**$137.894**	**$155.572**	**$177.237**	**$202.434**	**$122.0**

Emergency U.S. Stockpile in Israel

In the early 1980s, Israeli leaders sought to expand what they called their "strategic collaboration" with the United States military by allowing U.S. arms and equipment to be stockpiled at Israeli bases for use in wartime.[33] Nearly a decade later, the United States agreed to establish munitions stockpiles in Israel for use by the United States and, with U.S. permission, for use by Israel in emergency situations. The initial value of the U.S. material stored in Israel was set at $100 million. It increased over time, most recently to $800 million in 2010. The United States stores missiles, armored vehicles and artillery ammunition in Israel. According to one Israeli officer, "Officially, all of this equipment belongs to the US military…. If however, there is a conflict, the IDF can ask for permission to use some of the equipment."[34] During the 2006 war against Hezbollah in Lebanon, the United States granted Israel access to the stockpile.

Aid Restrictions and Possible Violations

Cluster Munitions

Although U.S. assistance to Israel has remained high for several decades, there have been some instances when the United States acted to restrict aid or rebuke Israel for possible improper use of U.S.-supplied military equipment. The 1952 Mutual Defense Assistance Agreement and subsequent arms agreements between Israel and the United States limit the use of U.S. military equipment to defensive purposes. The Arms Export Control Act states that the United States may stop aid to countries which use U.S. military assistance for purposes other than "legitimate self-defense." In 1982, the Reagan Administration determined that Israel "may" have violated its 1952 Mutual Defense Assistance Agreement with the United States by reportedly using U.S.-supplied anti-personnel cluster bombs against civilian targets during its military operations in Lebanon and

---

[33] "U.S.- Israel Strategic Link: Both Sides Take Stock," *New York Times*, October 2, 1981.

[34] "US may give Israel Iraq Ammo ," *Jerusalem Post*, February 11, 2010.

the siege of Beirut.[35] As a result, the Reagan Administration prohibited U.S. export of cluster bombs to Israel for six years.[36]

During the July-August 2006 war in Lebanon, Israel used cluster munitions to counter Hezbollah rocket attacks. The United States apparently supplied some of the cluster weapons that Israel used in the conflict.[37] Since the August 2006 Israeli-Hezbollah cease-fire, there have been a number of reported Lebanese civilian deaths and injuries from unexploded bomb remnants spread across a wide area of southern Lebanon.[38] After the war, the U.S. Department of State's Office of Weapons Removal and Abatement implemented a landmine and unexploded ordnance (UXO) humanitarian clearance program in Lebanon.

The Department of State's Directorate of Defense Trade Controls reportedly conducted an investigation focused on whether Israel violated confidential agreements with the United States that restrict Israel's use of U.S.-supplied cluster munitions to certain military targets in non-civilian areas. On January 28, 2007, the State Department issued a preliminary report to Congress concluding that Israel may have violated the terms of classified U.S.-Israeli procurement agreements on the use of cluster bombs in populated areas. According to then State Department spokesman Sean McCormack, "There were likely violations," though he added that "This is a preliminary finding and because it also involves the agreements about use (of munitions), which are classified, I cannot get into the details."[39] The State Department then asked Israel for additional information on reports that Israeli troops violated orders that restricted how U.S.-manufactured cluster bombs could be used during the summer 2006 war.[40]

In an April 2008 Senate Appropriations Subcommittee hearing, Senator Leahy asked then Secretary of State Condoleezza Rice if U.S.-supplied cluster munitions to Israel "were used in a manner that violated the export agreement on them." Secretary Rice responded by saying "Senator, I should probably get an answer to you. I remember that we investigated this matter. We talked to the Israelis about it.... It's a 'may have,' but I don't know where it is. But I will get to you as to where we are in those discussions.... We actually continue to have discussions with the Israelis about this and I know they've done a number of internal looks and investigations."[41]

Israel has conducted several investigations into its use of cluster munitions in the 2006 war in Lebanon. In December 2007, the Israel Defense Forces (IDF) concluded its investigation, stating

---

[35] See, CRS Report RL30982, *U.S. Defense Articles and Services Supplied to Foreign Recipients: Restrictions on Their Use*, by Richard F. Grimmett.

[36] The Reagan Administration also temporarily suspended the delivery of F-16 aircraft to Israel after it bombed the Iraqi nuclear reactor at Osirak in 1981.

[37] David S. Cloud, "Inquiry Opened Into Israeli Use Of U.S. Bombs," *New York Times* August 25, 2006. An August 26, 2006 presentation by United Nations Mine Action Coordination Center (UNMAS) South Lebanon office catalogued the following numbers of U.S.-manufactured cluster weapon sub-munitions during surveys in southern Lebanon (source weapons in parentheses): 715 M-42's (105-millimeter artillery shells), 820 M-77's (M-26 rockets), and 5 BLU-63's (CBU-26 cluster bombs). The UNMAS teams also reported 631 M-85 Israeli-produced sub-munitions had been found. See, UNMAS South Lebanon, "Cluster Bomb Situation - South Lebanon July/August 2006," August 26, 2006.

[38] According to the United Nations Mine Action Coordination Center (UNMACC), between 30% and 40% of Israeli-dropped cluster bombs failed to explode on impact. Israel claims that the "dud rate" was less than 15%.

[39] "U.S. Says Israel May Have Violated Agreement on Cluster Bomb Use," *Reuters*, January 29, 2007.

[40] "Israel May have Violated Arms Pact, U.S. Says," *New York Times*, January 28, 2007.

[41] Senate Appropriations Subcommittee on State, Foreign Operations, and Related Programs, Hearing on the Fiscal 2009 Budget for the State Department, April 9, 2008.

---

that "It was clear that the majority of the cluster munitions were fired at open and uninhabited areas, areas from which Hezbollah forces operated and in which no civilians were present.... The use of this weaponry was legal once it was determined that, in order to prevent rocket fire onto Israel, its use was a concrete military necessity." The IDF also announced that it would not press charges against officers who ordered the use of cluster bombs during the 2006 war. In February 2008, the Winograd Commission, a government-appointed Israeli commission of inquiry into the events of the 2006 war in Lebanon, concluded that "The facts regarding the use of cluster bombs demonstrated the faults in operational discipline, supervision and control and the lack of clarity of the commands and guidelines just as we had found in other aspects of the war. It is vital that the army learns the lessons that should be apparent from the use of cluster bombs during the war."[42]

In 2008, after several Israeli internal investigations and Congressional action[43] to attempt to restrict the overall export of U.S. cluster munitions, Israel announced that it would begin purchasing Israeli-made M85 cluster bombs rather than U.S.-manufactured bomblets. The M85 was developed by Israel Military Industries (IMI) and it is generally considered to be more reliable than U.S.-made cluster munitions. However, one Norwegian study asserted that the failure rate on the M85 was closer to 10% and not 1% as claimed by its proponents.[44]

Israeli Arms Transfers to Third Parties

As previously mentioned, Israel has become a major global leader in arms exports[45] and, over the last two decades, the United States and Israel have periodically disagreed over Israeli sales of sensitive U.S. and Israeli technologies to third party countries, most notably China. U.S. objections have largely been communicated by successive Administrations and Pentagon officials. In 2000, Representative Sonny Callahan, then-Chairman of the House Appropriations Subcommittee on Foreign Operations, sought to withhold $250 million in aid to Israel unless it cancelled a planned sale to China of an Airborne Early Warning System.[46] On June 20, 2000, the House Foreign Operations Subcommittee voted nine to six to defeat Callahan's proposal.[47] In

---

[42] "Army Urged to Review Inadequate Cluster Bomb Rules," *Jerusalem Post*, January 31, 2008.

[43] The FY2008 Consolidated Appropriations Act (P.L. 110-161) significantly restricted the export of U.S.-manufactured cluster munitions. Section 646(b) of the bill states that "no military assistance shall be furnished for cluster munitions, no defense export license for cluster munitions may be issued, and no cluster munitions or cluster munitions technology shall be sold or transferred, unless (1) the submunitions of the cluster munitions have a 99 percent or higher tested rate; and (2) the agreement applicable to the assistance, transfer, or sale of the cluster munitions or cluster munitions technology specifies that the cluster munitions will only be used against clearly defined military targets and will not be used where civilians are known to be present." On September 6, 2007, the President objected to efforts by lawmakers to ban the export of cluster munitions. In a statement of Administration policy, the President wrote, "The Administration also objects to restrictions on providing military assistance for cluster munitions.... Currently, the sales of cluster munitions are subject to safeguards. See, "Statement of Administration Policy, H.R. 2764 – State, Foreign Operations, and Related Programs Appropriations Act, 2008," Office of Management and Budget, September 6, 2007.

[44] M85, Analysis of Reliability, Available online at http://www.npaid.org/filestore/M85.pdf

[45] Israel's customers include Germany, Spain, France, Canada, Australia, Turkey, Singapore Brazil, India, Italy, the Netherlands, Poland and Romania.

[46] Eric Pianin, "Israel-China Radar Deal Opposed," *Washington Post*, April 7, 2000.

[47] According to the House Committee, "the Committee is very disturbed by reports that Israel is preparing to provide China with an airborne radar system that could threaten both the forces of democratic Taiwan and the United States in the region surrounding the Taiwan Strait. The Committee intends to revisit this issue as the appropriations process moves forward." H.Rept. 106-720, accompanying H.R. 4811 (P.L. 106-429), the FY2001 Foreign Operations Appropriations Act.

2005, the United States suspended Israel from participating in the development of the Joint Strike Fighter (JSF) and imposed other restrictions in defense ties because of Israeli plans to upgrade Chinese Harpy Killer drone aircraft. Israel ultimately canceled the sale.

In order to create a more transparent arms transfer process, former U.S. Defense Secretary Donald Rumsfeld and former Israeli Defense Minister Shaul Mofaz signed a 2005 bilateral agreement mandating Israeli consultation with the U.S. government on sensitive arms transfers to third parties. The Israeli government also has established its own arms export controls agency to supervise military sales. U.S. arms sales to Israel, like with all other recipients, are subject to stringent End-Use Monitoring (EUM) as mandated by the Arms Export Control Act (see Section 40A of P.L. 90-629 as amended).[48] Reports of canceled sales/negotiations include the following:

- In 2006, Israel reportedly froze a $100-million contract with Venezuela to upgrade its U.S.-manufactured F-16 fighter jets due to U.S. pressure. According to one former U.S. official, "We don't officially acknowledge our supervisory role or our de facto veto right over their exports.... It's a matter of courtesy to our Israeli friends, who are very serious about their sovereignty and in guarding their reputation on the world market."[49]

- In 2009, an Israeli defense company partnering with Swedish manufacturer Saab reportedly backed out of a tender competition to sell Swedish-designed fighter planes to India after the Pentagon expressed concern that American technology used by Israel would be integrated into the fighter.[50]

- In 2010, Israel suspended talks with Russia over the possible purchase of 12 reconnaissance Unmanned Aerial Vehicles (UAVs) in a contract worth potentially $50 million. Israel Aerospace Industries and Russia also were discussing the possible construction of a UAV manufacturing plant in Russia in a deal worth up to $200 million. The suspension could have been in response to Russian talks with Iran over transferring sophisticated air defense systems or to U.S. concerns over the transfer of advanced Israeli UAVs to Moscow. According to one report, the United States requested clarification about the deal.[51] On September 6, 2010, Russia and Israel signed a military cooperation agreement, though it is unclear whether it will lead to new Israeli sales of UAVs.

Israeli Settlements

Continued Israeli settlement building led the United States to reduce the amount of loan guarantees it has extended to Israel. By law, U.S. loan guarantees cannot be used to finance Israeli settlement building in areas occupied after the 1967 War. In the mid-1990s and then again in 2003 and 2005, the United States reduced loan guarantees to Israel by an amount equal to Israel's estimated spending on settlement construction in the West Bank and Gaza Strip (See **Table 3** below).

---

[48] 22 U.S.C. § 2785.

[49] "U.S. OKs Israel-China Spy Sat Deal," *DefenseNews.com*, October 12, 2007.

[50] "Israel Drops Indian Jets Venture under US Pressure: Report," *Agence France Presse*, July 6, 2009.

[51] "Military Sources: Jerusalem Blocking Multi-Million Russia Drone Deal," *Ha'aretz*, June 13, 2010.

Other Ongoing Assistance and Cooperative Programs

Migration & Refugee Assistance

Beginning in 1973, Israel has received grants from the State Department's Migration and Refugee Assistance fund (MRA)[52] to assist in the resettlement of migrants to Israel. Funds are paid to the United Israel Appeal, a private philanthropic organization in the United States, which in turn transfers the funds to the Jewish Agency for Israel.[53] Between 1973 and 1991, the United States gave about $460 million for resettling Jewish refugees in Israel. Annual amounts have varied from a low of $12 million to a high of $80 million, based on the number of Jews leaving the former Soviet Union and other areas for Israel. The Migration and Refugee funds for Israel are earmarked by Congress; the Administration usually does not request specific amounts of Migration and Refugee assistance for Israel.

Table 2. Migration and Refugee Assistance Funding Levels

FY2000:	$60 million
FY2001:	$60 million
FY2003:	$60 million
FY2004:	$59.6 million
FY2005:	$49.7 million
FY2006:	$50 million
FY2007:	$40 million
FY2008:	$40 million
FY2009:	$30 million
FY2010:	$25 million

Source: U.S. State Department.

Note: The level of funding reflects a decline in need due to the decreasing numbers of migrants to Israel.

Congress has changed the earmark language since the first refugee resettlement funds were appropriated in 1973. At first, the congressional earmark said the funds were for "resettlement in Israel of refugees from the Union of Soviet Socialist Republics and from Communist countries in Eastern Europe." But in 1985, the language was simplified to "refugees resettling in Israel" to ensure that Ethiopian Jews would be covered by the funding. Technically, the earmark designates funds for refugee resettlement, but in Israel little differentiation is made between "refugees" and other immigrants, and the funds are used to support the absorption of all immigrants.

---

[52] The Migration and Refugee Account (MRA) is authorized as part of the State Department funding but is appropriated through the Foreign Operations Appropriations bill.

[53] The Jewish Agency for Israel's website is available at http://www.jafi.org.il/.

Loan Guarantees

Overview

Since 1972, the United States has extended loan guarantees to Israel to assist with housing shortages, Israel's absorption of new immigrants from the former Soviet Union and Ethiopia, and its economic recovery following the 2000-2003 recession sparked by renewed Palestinian uprising. Loan guarantees are a form of indirect U.S. assistance to Israel, since they enable Israel to borrow from commercial sources at lower rates and not from the United States government. Congress directs that subsidies be set aside in a U.S. Treasury account for possible default. These subsidies, which are a percentage of the total loan (based in part on the credit rating of the borrowing country; in the case of the loan guarantees in the 1990s, the subsidy amount was 4.1%), have come from the U.S. or the Israeli government. Israel has never defaulted on a U.S.-backed loan guarantee, as it needs to maintain its good credit rating in order to secure financing to offset annual budget deficits.

Loan Guarantees for Economic Recovery

In 2003, then Prime Minister Ariel Sharon requested an additional $8 billion in loan guarantees to help Israel's failing economy. The loan guarantee request accompanied a request for an additional $4 billion in military grants to help Israel prepare for possible attacks during an anticipated U.S. war with Iraq and Israeli efforts to end the Palestinian uprising. P.L. 108-11, the FY2003 Emergency Wartime Supplemental Appropriations Act, authorized $9 billion in loan guarantees over three years for Israel's economic recovery and $1 billion in military grants. P.L. 108-11 stated that the proceeds from the loan guarantees could be used only within Israel's pre-June 5, 1967, borders; that the annual loan guarantees could be reduced by an amount equal to the amount Israel spends on settlements in the occupied territories; that Israel would pay all fees and subsidies; and that the President would consider Israel's economic reforms when determining terms and conditions for the loan guarantees. On November 26, 2003, the Department of State announced that the $3 billion loan guarantees for FY2003 were reduced by $289.5 million because Israel continued to build settlements in the occupied territories and continued construction of the security barrier separating Israelis and Palestinians. In FY2005, the U.S. government further reduced the amount available for Israel to borrow by an additional $795.8 million. Since then, no other deductions have been made.

According to the U.S. Treasury Department, Israel is legally obligated to use the proceeds of guaranteed loans for refinancing its government debt and also has agreed that proceeds shall not be used for military purposes or to support activities in areas outside its pre-June 5, 1967, borders. However, U.S. officials note that since Israel's national budget is fungible, proceeds from the issuance of U.S.-guaranteed debt that are used to refinance Israeli government debt free up domestic Israeli funds for other uses.[54]

P.L. 108-447, the FY2005 Consolidated Appropriations Act, first extended the authority of the loan guarantees from FY2005 to FY2007. In the aftermath of the 2006 Israel-Hezbollah conflict, President Bush stated that he would ask Congress to again extend the authorization of loan guarantees to Israel. P.L. 109-472, the 2006 Department of State Authorities Act, extended the

---

[54] CRS correspondence with the U.S. Treasury Department's Office of International Affairs, October 2009.

authority to provide loan guarantees through FY2011. Israel has not borrowed any funds since FY2005. In general, Israel may view U.S. loan guarantees as a "last resort" option, which its treasury could use if unguaranteed local and international bond issuances become too expensive.

In June 2009, the U.S.-Israel Joint Economic Development Group (JEDG) held its annual meeting. According to a U.S. Department of the Treasury press release, "The U.S. delegation commended Israel's strong economic performance and fiscal discipline in recent years. Both countries' delegations agreed to terms and conditions that will govern the U.S. Government's decision to make available FY2010 and FY2011 tranches of loan guarantees for use by Israel, subject to statutory deductions."[55]

Table 3. U.S. Loan Guarantees to Israel: FY2003-FY2012

($ in millions)

Fiscal Year	Amount Authorized and Allocated to Israel	Met U.S. Economic Reform Benchmarks?[a]	Deductions for Settlement Activity	Amount Borrowed by Israel	Amount Available for Israel to Borrow[b]
FY2003	3,000.0	Yes	289.5	1,600.0	1,110.5
FY2004	3,000.0	Yes	—	2,500.0	1,610.5
FY2005	1,000.0	Yes	795.8	—	1,814.7
FY2006	333.0	Conditions Waived due to war in Lebanon	—	—	2,148.0
FY2007	333.0	Yes	—	—	2,481.4
FY2008	333.0	Yes	—	—	2,814.7
FY2009	333.0	Conditions Waived due to global economic crisis	—	—	3,148.0
FY2010	333.0	n/a	n/a	n/a	n/a
FY2011	333.0	n/a	n/a	n/a	n/a

Source: U.S. Department of the Treasury and U.S. State Department

a. The United States and Israel have agreed that guarantees are not automatically available for use by Israel after they are authorized by the United States: per a June 2009 agreement, the United States must give written determination of the fulfillment (or waiver) of conditions before it releases tranches for use by Israel. The U.S.-Israel Joint Economic Development Group (JEDG) establishes benchmarks for Israel. These benchmarks contain conditions for deficit and spending caps, along with other fiscal and non-fiscal conditions.

b. Under current legislation, the loan guarantee program has a stated end of September 30, 2011; however, there is also a "carryover" provision in the statute under which Israel may draw on unused U.S. guarantees until September 30, 2012.

---

[55] U.S. Department of the Treasury, *U.S. – Israel Joint Economic Development Group Joint Statement*, TG-188, June 29, 2009.

American Schools and Hospitals Abroad Program (ASHA)[56]

Through Foreign Operations appropriations legislation, Congress has funded the ASHA program as part of the overall Development Assistance (DA) appropriation to the United States Agency for International Development (USAID). According to USAID, ASHA is designed to strengthen self-sustaining schools, libraries, and medical centers that best demonstrate American ideas and practices abroad. ASHA has been providing support to institutions in the Middle East since 1957, and a number of Israeli universities and hospitals have been recipients of ASHA grants. Over the past several years, Israeli institutions, such as the Shaare Zedek Medical Center in Jerusalem, The Feinberg Graduate School of the Weizmann Institute of Science, the Sackler Faculty of Medicine of the Tel Aviv University, The Hebrew University of Jerusalem, Bethlehem University, and the Hadassah Medical Organization, have received ASHA funding. The Hadassah Medical Organization was nominated for the 2005 Nobel Peace Prize for its equitable treatment of Palestinians and Israeli patients. According to USAID, institutions based in Israel have received the most program funding in the Middle East region.

Table 4. ASHA Program Grants to Israeli Institutions, FY2000-FY2009

Fiscal year	Amount
FY2000	$2.75 million
FY2001	$2.25 million
FY2002	$2.65 million
FY2003	$3.05 million
FY2004	$3.15 million
FY2005	$2.95 million
FY2006	$3.35 million
FY2007	$2.95 million
FY2008	$3.90 million
FY2009	$3.90 million
Total	**$30.9 million**

Source: USAID.

U.S.-Israeli Scientific & Business Cooperation

In the early 1970s, Israeli academics and businessmen began looking for ways to expand investment in Israel's high technology sector. At the time, Israel's nascent technology sector, which would later become the driving force in Israel's economy, was in need of private capital for research and development. The United States and Israel launched several programs to stimulate

---

[56] According to USAID, recipients of ASHA grants on behalf of overseas institutions must be private U.S. organizations, headquartered in the United States, and tax-exempt. The U.S. organization must also serve as the founder for and/or sponsor of the overseas institution. Schools must be for secondary or higher education and hospital centers must conduct medical education and research outside the United States. Grants are made to U.S. sponsors for the exclusive benefit of institutions abroad. See http://www.usaid.gov/our_work/cross-cutting_programs/asha/.

Israeli industrial and scientific research, and Congress has on several occasions authorized and appropriated funds for the following organizations:

- The BIRD Foundation (Israel-U.S. Binational Research & Development Foundation).[57] BIRD, which was established in 1977, provides matchmaking services between Israeli and American companies in research and development with the goal of expanding cooperation between U.S. and Israeli private high tech industries.

- The BSF Foundation (U.S.-Israel Binational Science Foundation).[58] BSF, which was started in 1972, promotes cooperation in scientific and technological research.

- The BARD Foundation (Binational Agriculture and Research and Development Fund). BARD was created in 1978 and supports U.S.-Israeli cooperation in agricultural research.[59]

Section 917 of P.L. 110-140, the Renewable Fuels, Consumer Protection, and Energy Efficiency Act of 2007, contains the original language of the U.S.-Israel Energy Cooperation Act (H.R. 1838). Although it does not appropriate any funds for joint research and development, it does establish a grant program to support research, development, and commercialization of renewable energy or energy efficiency. The law also authorizes the Secretary of Energy to provide funds for the grant program as needed.

Congress appropriates funds for the U.S.-Israeli Energy Cooperation Program in the annual Energy and Water Development and Related Agencies Appropriations bill. In FY2009, Congress provided $2 million for the program in P.L. 111-8, the Omnibus Appropriations Act, 2009.[60] In FY2010, Congress provided an additional $2 million in P.L. 111-85, the Energy and Water Development and Related Agencies Appropriations Act, 2010.

In November 2009, the U.S. Department of Energy and the Israeli Ministry of National Infrastructures announced that they would each contribute $3.3 million to the BIRD Foundation to launch four clean energy projects. The projects include two solar power related technologies, a "smart grid" technology and a biodiesel project.

In January 2010, the Israeli government injected an additional $55 million into the BIRD, BSF, and BARD foundations. According to Israeli Finance Minister Yuval Steinitz, "This is a

---

[57] See http://www.birdf.com/default.asp. Congress helped establish BIRD's endowment with appropriations of $30 million and $15 million in 1977 and 1985 respectively. These grants were matched by the Israeli government for a total endowment of $90 million.

[58] See http://www.bsf.org.il/Gateway4/. Congress helped establish BSF's endowment with appropriations of $30 million and $20 million in 1972 and 1984 respectively. These grants were matched by Israel for a total endowment of $100 million. According to the treaty establishing the Foundation, the Foundation shall use the interest, as well as any funds derived from its activities, for the operations of the Foundation.

[59] See http://www.bard-isus.com/. Congress helped establish BARD's endowment with appropriations of $40 million and $15 million in 1979 and 1985 respectively. These grants were matched by the State of Israel for a total endowment of $110 million. In recent years, Congress has provided funds for BARD in annual Agriculture Appropriations legislation at approximately $500,000 a year.

[60] P.L. 111-8 did not specify an amount for the program but adopted the House version of the energy and water appropriations bill that recommended $2 million to fund the U.S.-Israeli cooperative agreement. The Senate version had recommended $5 million for FY2009.

---

significant and important step for strengthening economic and technological ties with the United States and for capital inflows to Israeli innovation.... We hope that in the wake of this step, we will find more opportunities for achieving these targets."

Historical Background

1948-1970

U.S. government assistance to Israel began in 1949 with a $100 million Export-Import Bank Loan.[61] For the next two decades, U.S. aid to Israel was modest and was far less than in later years.[62] Although the United States provided moderate amounts of economic aid (mostly loans), Israel's main early patron was France, which provided Israel with advanced military equipment and technology.[63] In 1962, Israel purchased its first advanced weapons system from the United States (Hawk antiaircraft missiles).[64] In 1968, a year after Israel's victory in the Six Day War in June 1967, the Johnson Administration, with strong support from Congress, approved the sale of Phantom aircraft to Israel, establishing the precedent for U.S. support for what later came to be referred to as Israel's qualitative military edge over its neighbors.[65]

1970-Present

Large-scale U.S. assistance for Israel increased considerably after Arab-Israeli wars created a sense among many Americans that Israel was continually under siege.[66] Consequently, Congress, supported by broad U.S. public opinion, committed to strengthening Israel's military and economy through large increases in foreign aid. From 1966 through 1970, average aid per year increased to about $102 million and military loans increased to about 47% of the total. In 1971, the United States provided Israel with military loans of $545 million, up from $30 million in 1970. Also in 1971, Congress first designated a specific amount of aid for Israel in legislation (an "earmark"). Economic assistance changed from project aid, such as support for agricultural development work, to a Commodity Import Program (CIP) for the purchase of U.S. goods.[67] In effect, the United States stepped in to fill the role that France had relinquished after French

---

[61] In 1948, President Harry Truman, who sympathized with the plight of Israel in its early days and recognized its statehood over the objections of some of his top advisors, placed an arms embargo on Israel and her Arab neighbors in order to keep the United States neutral in the ongoing Arab-Israeli conflict. The Tripartite Declaration of 1950 reaffirmed U.S., British, and French opposition to the development of Arab-Israeli arms races.

[62] From 1949 through 1965, U.S. aid to Israel averaged about $63 million per year, over 95% of which was economic development assistance and food aid. A modest military loan program began in 1959.

[63] France supplied Israel with military equipment mainly to counter Egypt. In the 1950s and early 1960s, Egypt antagonized France by providing arms and training for Algeria's war for independence against France.

[64] "America's Staunchest Mideast Ally," *Christian Science Monitor*, August 21, 2003.

[65] Section 303 of P.L. 90-554, *Foreign Assistance Act of 1968*, expresses the sense of Congress to see the United States negotiate the sale of supersonic aircraft to Israel.

[66] Between 1967 and 1973, Israel and its Arab neighbors fought the June 1967 War, the ensuing War of Attrition (1969), and the October 1973 War. Israel also was engaged in low level guerrilla warfare with the Palestinian Liberation Organization and other groups, which had bases in Jordan and later in Lebanon. The 1974 emergency aid for Israel, following the 1973 war, included the first U.S. military grant aid to Israel.

[67] The Commodity Import Program for Israel ended in 1979 and was replaced with direct, largely unconditional cash transfers.

President Charles de Gaulle refused to supply Israel with military hardware to protest its preemptive launch of the Six Day War in June 1967. Israel became the largest recipient of U.S. foreign assistance in 1974. From 1971 to the present, U.S. aid to Israel has averaged over $2.6 billion per year, two-thirds of which has been military assistance.

1979 Israeli-Egyptian Peace Treaty

The 1979 Camp David Peace Treaty between Israel and Egypt ushered in the current era of U.S. financial support for peace between Israel and her Arab neighbors. To facilitate a full and formal cessation of hostilities and Israel's return of the Sinai Peninsula, the United States provided a total of $7.5 billion to both parties in 1979. The "Special International Security Assistance Act of 1979" (P.L. 96-35) provided military and economic grants to Israel and Egypt at a ratio of 3:2, respectively.[68]

Emergency Aid

U.S. assistance also has been used to help ease financial pressures on the Israeli treasury during recession.[69] In 1985, the United States significantly increased U.S. assistance to Israel, with Congress passing a special economic assistance package of $1.5 billion in order to help the Israeli economy cope with soaring inflation and economic stagnation.[70] As part of the assistance agreement, the United States and Israel formed the U.S.-Israel Joint Economic Development Group (JEDG) in order to support Israeli economic reforms.[71] In addition, all U.S. military aid to Israel was converted into grants in 1985.[72] U.S. economic aid had been converted to a cash grant transfer in 1981.

During times of domestic unrest in Israel and regional instability, U.S. aid to Israel has increased. In 1991, Congress provided Israel $650 million in emergency grants to pay for damage and other costs from Operation Desert Storm. In addition, Israel was given Patriot missiles to defend against Iraqi Scud missile attacks. After the 1991 collapse of the Soviet Union and the ensuing increase in migration of Russian and other Eastern bloc Jews to Israel, Congress approved $10 billion in loan guarantees for Israel to help it absorb immigrants and provide them with adequate social services. Finally, in the aftermath of the 2003 Iraq invasion, Congress passed the FY2003 Emergency Supplemental Appropriations Act (P.L. 108-11), which included $9 billion in loan guarantees over three years for Israel's economic recovery and $1 billion in military grants.

---

[68] This ratio is not found in the text of the 1978 and 1979 Camp David agreements. U.S. officials have not formally recognized the ratio. Egypt believes that, since it took political risks in making peace with Israel, the United States should be even-handed in its assistance policy to the region. The Egyptian government claims that a 3:2 ratio between Israel and Egypt was established during the negotiations.

[69] Beginning in the mid-1970s, Israel could no longer meet its balance of payments and government deficits with imported capital (gifts from overseas Jews, West German reparations, U.S. aid) and began to rely more on borrowed capital. Growing debt servicing costs, mounting government social services expenditures, perennial high defense spending, and a stagnant domestic economy combined with worldwide inflation and declining foreign markets for Israeli goods to push the Israeli economy into a near crisis situation in the mid-1980s.

[70] See Title I, Chapter V of P.L. 99-88, Economic Support Fund Assistance for Israel, Egypt, and Jordan. In 1985, the United States and Israel also concluded a Free Trade Agreement, which dramatically boosted Israeli exports to the United States.

[71] The JEDG meets on an annual basis to discuss financial sector and labor market reforms, trade liberalization, and privatization. The JEDG also monitors the disbursement of U.S. loan guarantees to Israel.

[72] The 1974 emergency aid for Israel, following the 1973 war, included the first military grant aid.

Using Aid to Support the Peace Process

During the 1990s, the United States provided aid to support the Israeli-Palestinian peace process. In late 1998, Israel requested $1.2 billion in additional U.S. aid to fund the movement of troops and military installations out of areas of the West Bank as called for in the October 23, 1998 Wye Agreement.[73] The Clinton Administration requested $1.2 billion in military aid for Israel to implement the Wye Agreement despite the fact that its implementation had stalled. President Clinton vetoed H.R. 2606, the FY2000 foreign operations appropriations bill, in part because it did not include the Wye funding. On November 29, 1999, the President signed the consolidated appropriations bill, H.R. 3194 (P.L. 106-113), which included in Division B passage of H.R. 3422, the Foreign Operations Appropriations bill. Title VI of H.R. 3422 included the $1.2 billion Wye funding for Israel.

---

[73] The full text of the 1998 Wye River Memorandum, a U.S.-brokered Israeli-Palestinian security agreement, is available online at http://www.mfa.gov.il/NR/exeres/EE54A289-8F0A-4CDC-93C9-71BD631109AB.htm.

Appendix. Recent Aid to Israel

Table A-1 shows cumulative U.S. aid to Israel for FY1949 through FY1996, and U.S. aid to Israel for each fiscal year since. Detail for the years 1949-1996 is shown in **Table A-2**.

Table A-1. Recent U.S. Aid to Israel

(millions of dollars)

Year	Total	Military Grant	Economic Grant	Immig. Grant	ASHA	All other
1949-1996	68,030.9	29,014.9	23,122.4	868.9	121.4	14,903.3
1997	3,132.1	1,800.0	1,200.0	80.0	2.1	50.0
1998	3,080.0	1,800.0	1,200.0	80.0	—	—
1999	3,010.0	1,860.0	1,080.0	70.0	—	—
2000	4,131.85	3,120.0	949.1	60.0	2.75	—
2001	2,876.05	1,975.6	838.2	60.0	2.25	—
2002	2,850.65	2,040.0	720.0	60.0	2.65	28.0
2003	3,745.15	3,086.4	596.1	59.6	3.05	—
2004	2,687.25	2,147.3	477.2	49.7	3.15	9.9
2005	2,612.15	2,202.2	357.0	50.0	2.95	—
2006	2,534.5	2,257.0	237.0	40.0	—	0.5
2007	2,503.15	2,340.0	120.0	40.0	2.95	0.2
2008	2,423.9	2,380.0	0	40.0	3.90	0
2009	2,583.9	2,550.0	0	30.0	3.90	0
2010	2,800.0	2,775.0	0	25.0	—	0
Total	**109,001.55**	**61,348.4**	**30,897.0**	**1,613.2**	**151.05**	**14,991.9**

Notes: ESF was earmarked for $960 million for FY2000 but was reduced to meet a 0.38% recision. FY2000 military grants include $1.2 billion for the Wye agreement and $1.92 billion in annual military aid. Final amounts for FY2003 are reduced by 0.65% mandated recision, and final amounts for FY2004 are reduced by 0.59%.

The $600 million in housing loan guarantees, $5.5 billion in military debt reduction loan guarantees, $9.2 billion in Soviet Jew resettlement loan guarantees, and $9 billion in economic recovery loan guarantees are not included in the tables because the United States government did not transfer funds to Israel. The United States underwrote loans to Israel from commercial institutions.

Table A-2. U.S. Assistance to Israel, FY1949-FY1996

(millions of dollars)

Year	Total	Military Loan	Military Grant	Economic Loan	Economic Grant	FFP Loan	FFP Grant
1949	100.0	-	-	-	-	-	-
1950	-	-	-	-	-	-	-
1951	35.1	-	-	-	0.1	-	-
1952	86.4	-	-	-	63.7	-	22.7
1953	73.6	-	-	-	73.6	-	a
1954	74.7	-	-	-	54.0	-	20.7
1955	52.7	-	-	20.0	21.5	10.8	0.4
1956	50.8	-	-	10.0	14.0	25.2	1.6
1957	40.9	-	-	10.0	16.8	11.8	2.3
1958	85.4	-	-	15.0	9.0	34.9	2.3
1959	53.3	0.4	-	10.0	9.2	29.0	1.7
1960	56.2	0.5	-	15.0	8.9	26.8	4.5
1961	77.9	a	-	16.0	8.5	13.8	9.8
1962	93.4	13.2	-	45.0	0.4	18.5	6.8
1963	87.9	13.3	-	45.0	-	12.4	6.0
1964	37.0	-	-	20.0	-	12.2	4.8
1965	65.1	12.9	-	20.0	-	23.9	4.9
1966	126.8	90.0	-	10.0	-	25.9	0.9
1967	23.7	7.0	-	5.5	-	-	0.6
1968	106.5	25.0	-	-	-	51.3	0.5
1969	160.3	85.0	-	-	-	36.1	0.6
1970	93.6	30.0	-	-	-	40.7	0.4
1971	634.3	545.0	-	-	-	55.5	0.3
1972	430.9	300.0	-	-	50.0	53.8	0.4
1973	492.8	307.5	-	-	50.0	59.4	0.4
1974	2,621.3	982.7	1,500.0	-	50.0	-	1.5
1975	778.0	200.0	100.0	-	344.5	8.6	-
1976	2,337.7	750.0	750.0	225.0	475.0	14.4	a
TQ	292.5	100.0	100.0	25.0	50.0	3.6	-
1977	1,762.5	500.0	500.0	245.0	490.0	7.0	-
1978	1,822.6	500.0	500.0	260.0	525.0	6.8	-
1979	4,888.0	2,700.0	1,300.0	260.0	525.0	5.1	-
1980	2,121.0	500.0	500.0	260.0	525.0	1.0	-
1981	2,413.4	900.0	500.0	-	764.0	-	-
1982	2,250.5	850.0	550.0	-	806.0	-	-

Year	Total	Military Loan	Military Grant	Economic Loan	Economic Grant	FFP Loan	FFP Grant
1983	2,505.6	950.0	750.0	-	785.0	-	-
1984	2,631.6	850.0	850.0	-	910.0	-	-
1985	3,376.7	-	1,400.0	-	1,950.0	-	
1986	3,663.5	-	1,722.6	-	1,898.4	-	-
1987	3,040.2	-	1,800.0	-	1,200.0	-	-
1988	3,043.4	-	1,800.0	-	1,200.0	-	-
1989	3,045.6	-	1,800.0	-	1,200.0	-	-
1990	3,034.9	-	1,792.3	-	1,194.8	-	-
1991	3,712.3	-	1,800.0	-	1,850.0	-	-
1992	3,100.0	-	1,800.0	-	1,200.0	-	-
1993	3,103.4	-	1,800.0	-	1,200.0	-	-
1994	3,097.2	-	1,800.0	-	1,200.0	-	-
1995	3,102.4	-	1,800.0	-	1,200.0	-	-
1996	3,144.0	-	1,800.0	-	1,200.0	-	-
Total	**68,030.9**	**11,212.5**	**29,014.9**	**1,516.5**	**23,122.4**	**588.5**	**94.1**

Year	Ex-Im. Bank Loan	Jewish Refug. Resettle Grant	Amer. Schools & Hosp. Grant	Other Loan	Coop. Devel. Grant	Other Grant
1949	100.0	-	-	-	-	-
1950	-	-	-	-	-	-
1951	35.0	-	-	-	-	-
1952	-	-	-	-	-	-
1953	-	-	-	-	-	-
1954	-	-	-	-	-	-
1955	-	-	-	-	-	-
1956	-	-	-	-	-	-
1957	-	-	-	-	-	-
1958	24.2	-	-	-	-	-
1959	3.0	-	-	-	-	-
1960	0.5	-	-	-	-	-
1961	29.8	-	-	-	-	-
1962	9.5	-	-	-	-	-
1963	11.2	-	-	-	-	-
1964	-	-	-	-	-	-
1965	3.4	-	-	-	-	-
1966	-	-	-	-	-	-
1967	9.6	-	1.0	-	-	-

Year	Ex-Im. Bank Loan	Jewish Refug. Resettle Grant	Amer. Schools & Hosp. Grant	Other Loan	Coop. Devel. Grant	Other Grant
1968	23.7	-	6.0	-	-	-
1969	38.6	-	-	-	-	-
1970	10.0	-	12.5	-	-	-
1971	31.0	-	2.5	-	-	-
1972	21.1	-	5.6	-	-	-
1973	21.1	50.0	4.4	-	-	-
1974	47.3	36.5	3.3	-	-	-
1975	62.4	40.0	2.5	-	-	20.0
1976	104.7	15.0	3.6	-	-	-
TQ	12.6	-	1.3	-	-	-
1977	0.9	15.0	4.6	-	-	-
1978	5.4	20.0	5.4	-	-	-
1979	68.7	25.0	4.2	-	-	-
1980	305.9	25.0	4.1	-	-	-
1981	217.4	25.0	2.0	-	5.0	-
1982	6.5	12.5	3.0	17.5	5.0	-
1983	-	12.5	3.1	-	5.0	-
1984	-	12.5	4.1	-	5.0	-
1985	-	15.0	4.7	-	7.0	-
1986	15.0	12.0	5.5	-	10.0	-
1987	-	25.0	5.2	-	10.0	-
1988	-	25.0	4.9	-	13.5	-
1989	-	28.0	6.9	-	10.7	-
1990	-	29.9	3.5	-	14.4	-
1991	-	45.0	2.6	-	14.7	-
1992	-	80.0	3.5	-	16.5	-
1993	-	80.0	2.5	-	20.9	-
1994	-	80.0	2.7	-	14.5	-
1995	-	80.0	2.9	-	19.5	-
1996	-	80.0	3.3	-	14.0	50.0
Total	**1218.5**	**868.9**	**121.4**	**17.5**	**185.7**	**70.0**

Notes: a = less than $50,000

- = None

NA = Not Available

TQ = Transition Quarter, when the U.S. fiscal year changed from June to September.

FFP = Food for Peace

Cooperative Development Grant: Three programs are in the cooperative development category: Middle East Regional Cooperation (MERC) intended for projects that foster economic growth and economic cooperation between Israel and its neighbors; Cooperative Development Program (CDP); and the Cooperative Development

Research (CDR), both of which fund Israel's foreign aid program. Israel received about one half of the $94 million MERC, and all of the $53 million CDP and $39 million CDR.

"Other Loan" is a CCC loan. "Other Grants" are $20 million in 1975 for a seawater desalting plant and $50 million in 1996 for anti-terrorism.

Definition of Aid: Under the category of foreign aid, some people include other funds transferred to Israel, such as the $180 million for research and development of the Arrow missile, or the $7.9 billion in loan guarantees for housing or settling Soviet Jews in Israel. None of these funds is included in this table.

Author Contact Information

Jeremy M. Sharp
Specialist in Middle Eastern Affairs
jsharp@crs.loc.gov, 7-8687